GOLF
FUNNY QUOTES & CLEVER CONCLUSIONS

I golf for my own entertainment and my teammates' entertainment.

Hilary Knight

Golf, like measles,
should be caught
young.

P. G. Wodehouse

Acting is like golf:
analysis leads to
paralysis.

Peter Falk

I still don't get golf.

Lance Armstrong

Fame is addictive.
Money is addictive.
Attention is
addictive. But golf is
second to none.

Marc Anthony

Golf and dating
don't mix.

Larry David

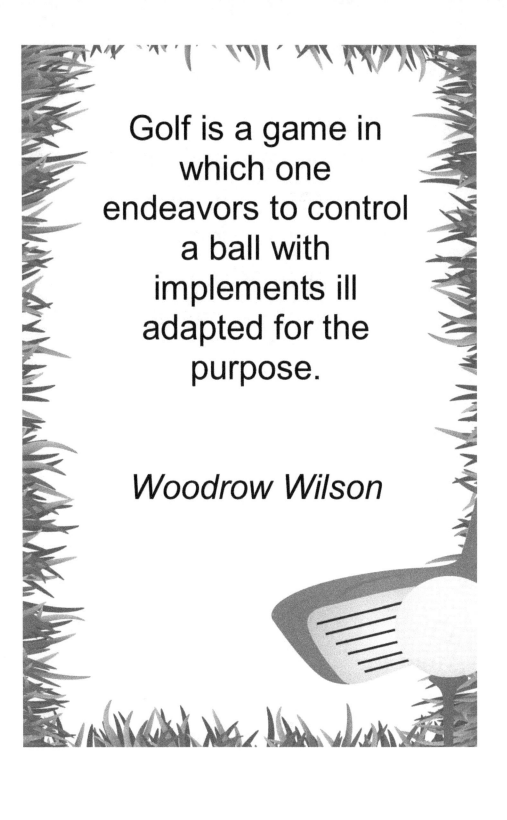

Golf is a game in which one endeavors to control a ball with implements ill adapted for the purpose.

Woodrow Wilson

Golf is an awkward set of bodily contortions designed to produce a graceful result.

Tommy Armour

Golf is like solitaire.
When you cheat,
you only cheat
yourself.

Tony Lema

The only way to enjoy golf is to be a masochist. Go out and beat yourself to death.

Howard Keel

Golf is such a
wonderful game.
I love it to death.

Charlie Sifford

I like boring golf.
That's kind of what
butters my bread.

Zach Johnson

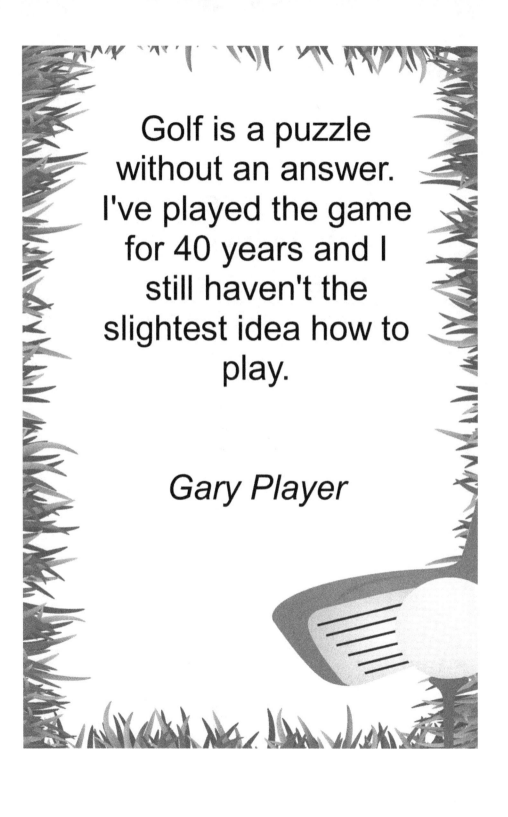

Golf is a puzzle
without an answer.
I've played the game
for 40 years and I
still haven't the
slightest idea how to
play.

Gary Player

For me, the worst part of playing golf, by far, has always been hitting the ball.

Dave Barry

Golf is meaningless,
but it means so
much.

Dennis Quaid

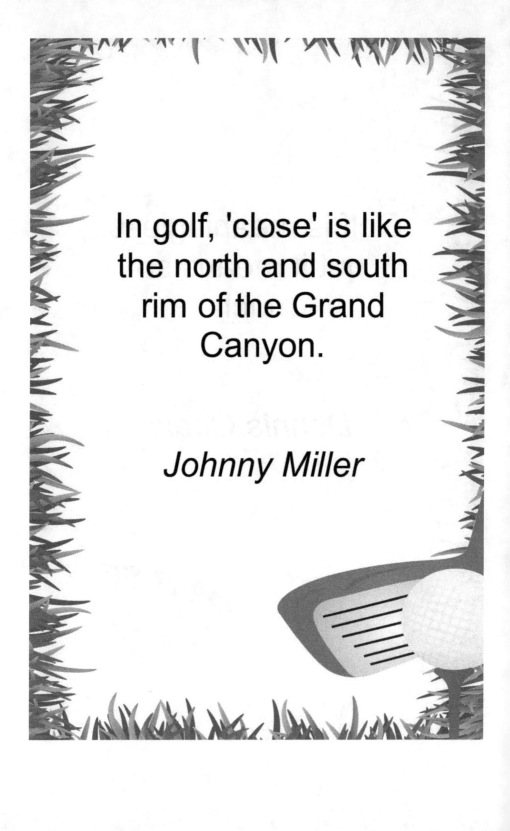

In golf, 'close' is like the north and south rim of the Grand Canyon.

Johnny Miller

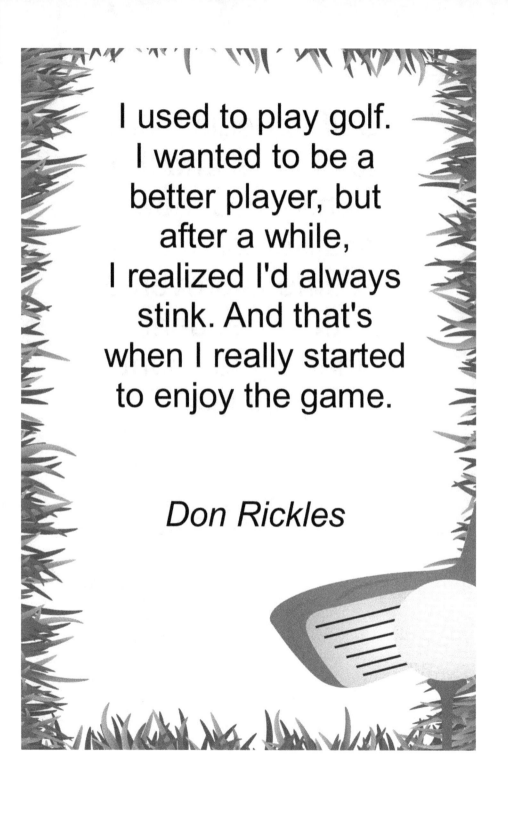

I used to play golf.
I wanted to be a
better player, but
after a while,
I realized I'd always
stink. And that's
when I really started
to enjoy the game.

Don Rickles

Golf appeals to the idiot in us and the child. Just how childlike golf players become is proven by their frequent inability to count past five.

John Updike

Golf is more fun than walking naked in a strange place, but not much.

Buddy Hackett

Exercise? I get it on
the golf course.
When I see my
friends collapse,
I run for the
paramedics.

Red Skelton

If he's got golf clubs in his truck or a camper in his driveway, I don't hire him.

Lou Holtz

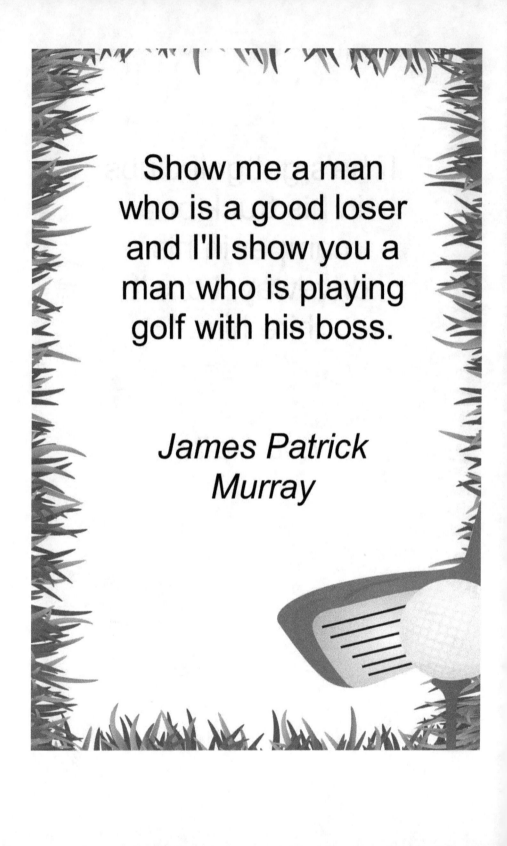

Show me a man
who is a good loser
and I'll show you a
man who is playing
golf with his boss.

*James Patrick
Murray*

They call it golf
because all the other
four letter words
were taken.

Raymond Floyd

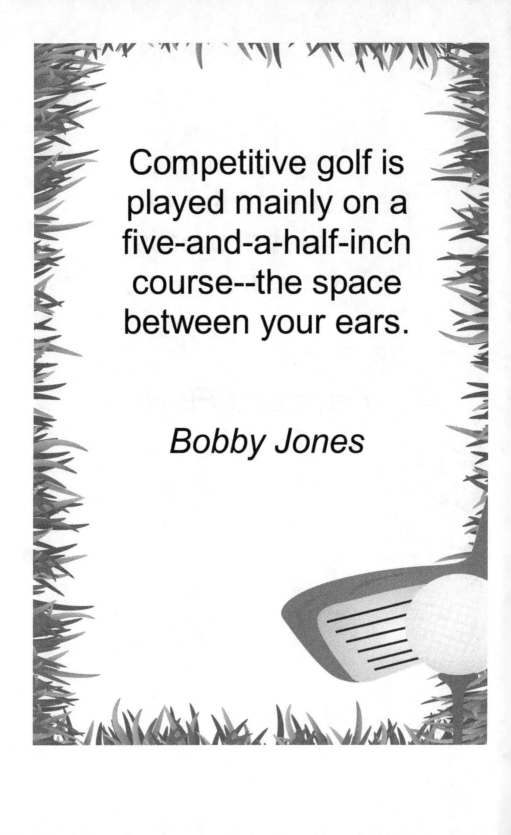

Competitive golf is played mainly on a five-and-a-half-inch course--the space between your ears.

Bobby Jones

One thing that golf
teaches you is
humility.

Robert Wagner

Golf is a game in which you yell 'fore,' shoot six, and write down five.

Paul Harvey

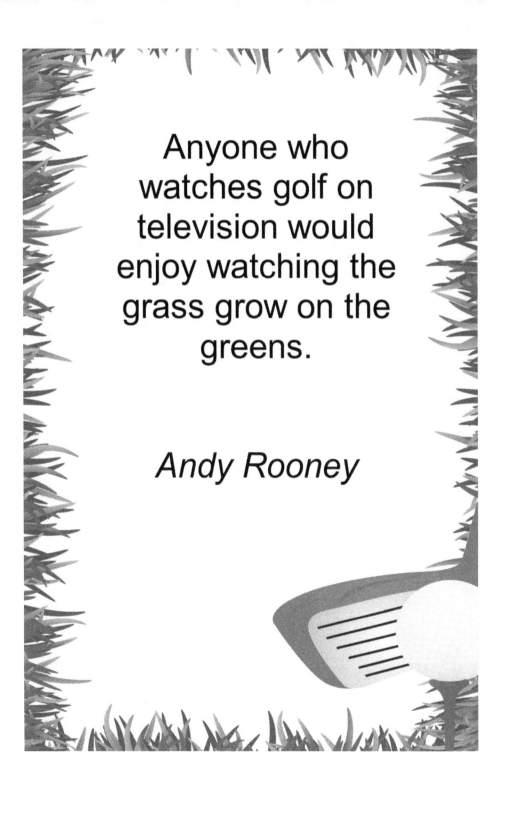

Anyone who watches golf on television would enjoy watching the grass grow on the greens.

Andy Rooney

I regard golf as an expensive way of playing marbles.

Gilbert K. Chesterton

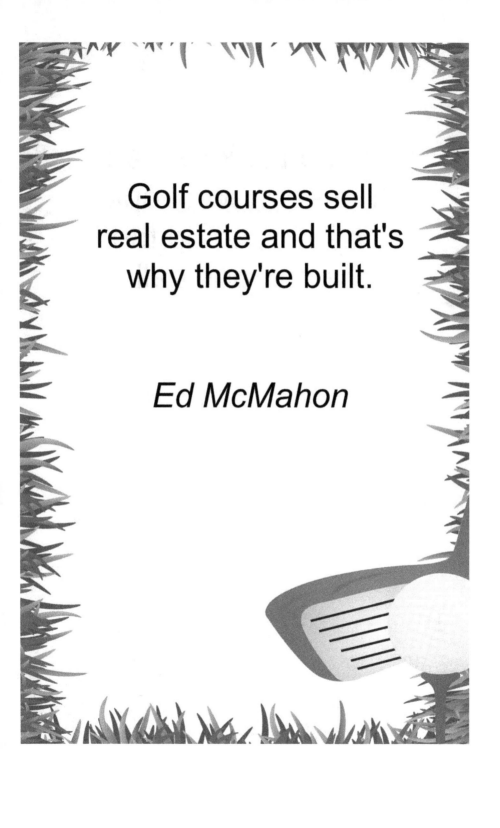

Golf courses sell
real estate and that's
why they're built.

Ed McMahon

If you think it's hard
to meet new people,
try picking up the
wrong golf ball.

Jack Lemmon

The object of golf is not just to win. It is to play like a gentleman, and win.

Phil Mickelson

Professional golf is the only sport where, if you win 20% of the time, you're the best.

Jack Nicklaus

Golf is deceptively
simple and endlessly
complicated.

Arnold Palmer

Golf balls are sweet: dimpled and sometimes even smiling.

Steve Rushin

Tennis and golf are
best played,
not watched.

Roger Kahn

My golf is woeful but
I will never
surrender.

Bing Crosby

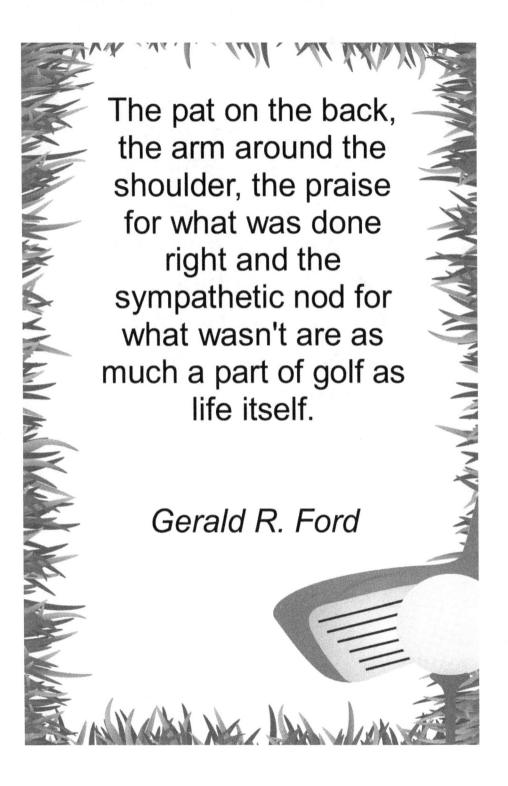

The pat on the back, the arm around the shoulder, the praise for what was done right and the sympathetic nod for what wasn't are as much a part of golf as life itself.

Gerald R. Ford

Golf is the infallible test. The man who can go into a patch of rough alone, with the knowledge that only God is watching him, and play his ball where it lies, is the man who will serve you faithfully and well.

P. G. Wodehouse

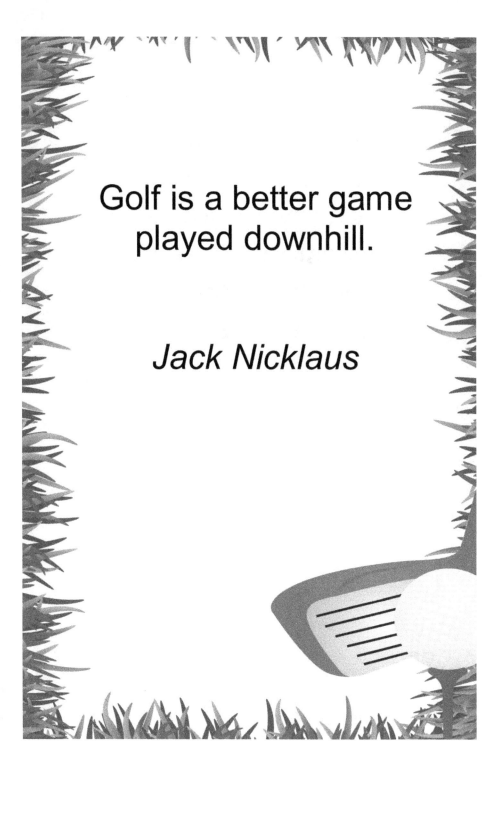

Golf is a better game
played downhill.

Jack Nicklaus

Although golf was originally restricted to wealthy, overweight Protestants, today it's open to anybody who owns hideous clothing.

Dave Barry

The golf ball has no sense at all, which is why it has to be given stern lectures constantly, especially during the act of putting.

Dan Jenkins

Though we endow them with human features - heads, faces, heels, toes - golf clubs are profoundly inhuman tools.

Steve Rushin

People always say golfers don't smile. But there is so much psychology in golf so we have to be a bit robotic.

Lee Westwood

You know, the Oscar I was awarded for **The Untouchables** is a wonderful thing, but I can honestly say that I'd rather have won the U.S. Open Golf Tournament.

Sean Connery

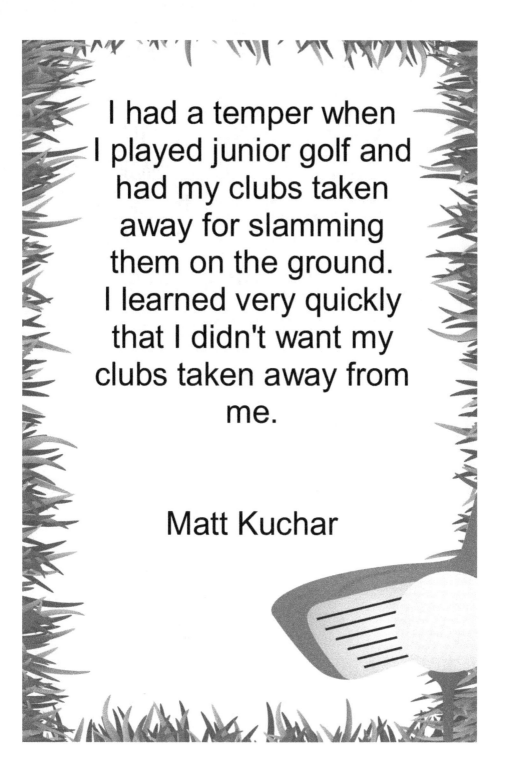

I had a temper when I played junior golf and had my clubs taken away for slamming them on the ground. I learned very quickly that I didn't want my clubs taken away from me.

Matt Kuchar

Golf is a game with morals. There's always an opportunity to be a scoundrel. That's why it's a gentleman's game.

Katt Williams

I don't believe in luck.
Not in golf, anyway.
There are good bounces
and bad bounces, sure,
but the ball is round and
so is the hole. If you find
yourself in a position
where you hope for luck
to pull you through,
you're in serious trouble.

Jack Nicklaus

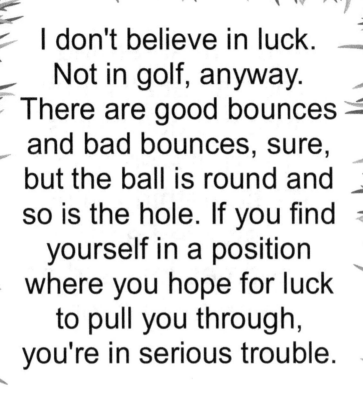

You must remind yourself at all times that the golf ball is nothing. It's an object. It's something to be swatted and sometimes lost and not even looked for.

Dan Jenkins

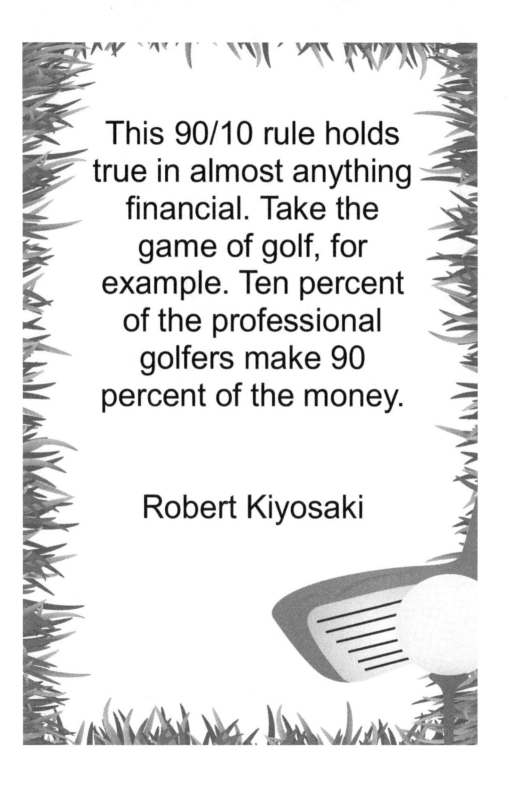

This 90/10 rule holds true in almost anything financial. Take the game of golf, for example. Ten percent of the professional golfers make 90 percent of the money.

Robert Kiyosaki

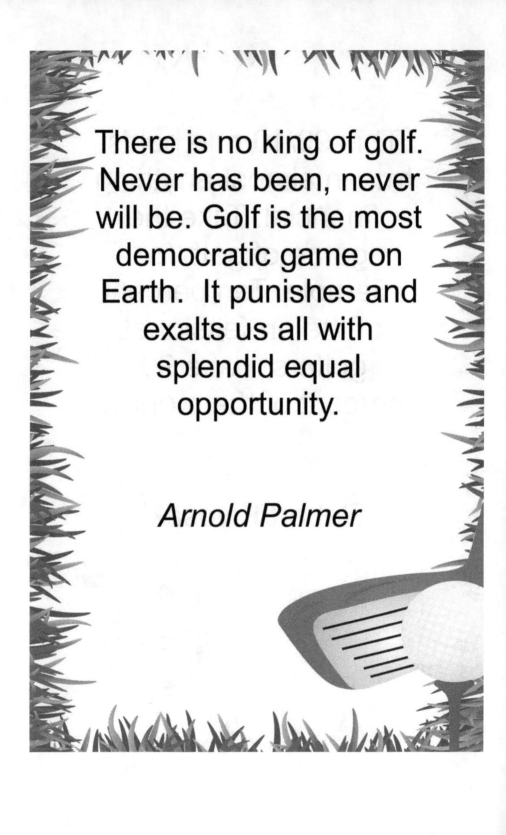

There is no king of golf. Never has been, never will be. Golf is the most democratic game on Earth. It punishes and exalts us all with splendid equal opportunity.

Arnold Palmer

I learned one thing from jumping motorcycles that was of great value on the golf course, the putting green especially: Whatever you do, don't come up short.

Evel Knievel

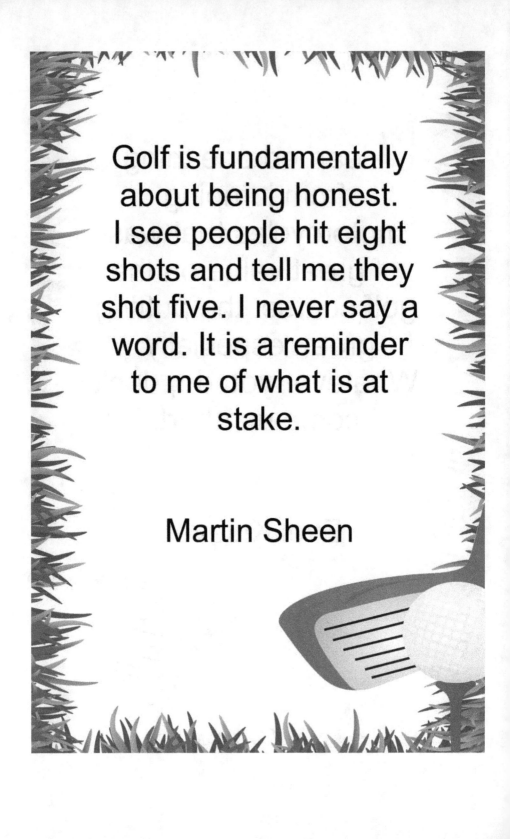

Golf is fundamentally about being honest. I see people hit eight shots and tell me they shot five. I never say a word. It is a reminder to me of what is at stake.

Martin Sheen

The difference between men and women seems to be this: I can argue with my promoter downstairs, accuse him of ripping me off, and 20 minutes later we'll be playing golf together. With a lady, the same argument can go on for, like, years.

David Hasselhoff

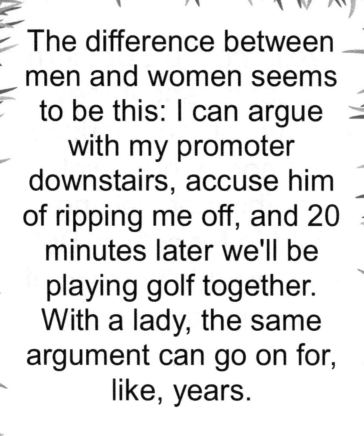

Well, they're Southern people, and if they know you are working at home they think nothing of walking right in for coffee. But they wouldn't dream of interrupting you at golf.

Harper Lee

A golf course is
nothing but a pool
room moved
outdoors.

Frank Butler

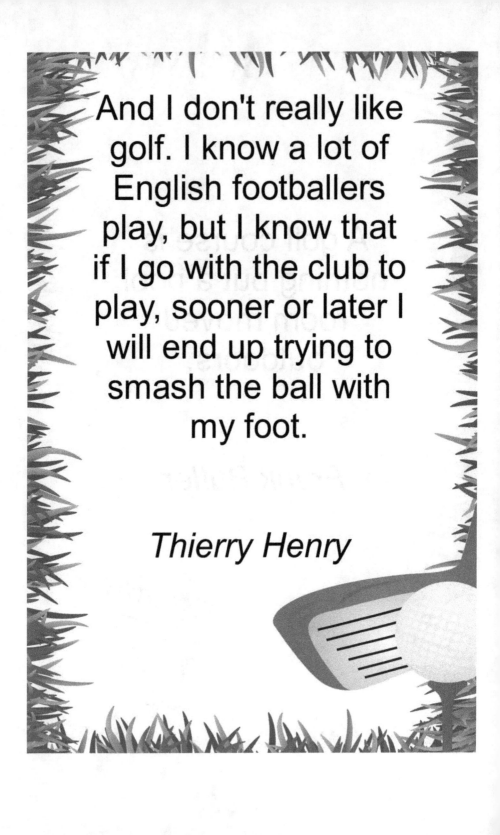

And I don't really like golf. I know a lot of English footballers play, but I know that if I go with the club to play, sooner or later I will end up trying to smash the ball with my foot.

Thierry Henry

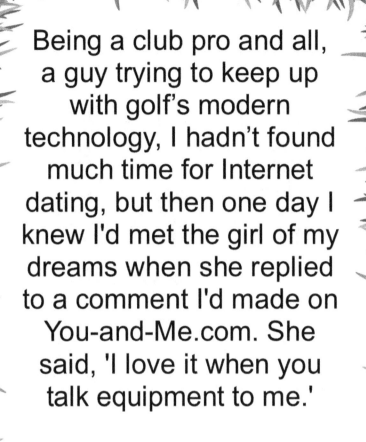

Being a club pro and all, a guy trying to keep up with golf's modern technology, I hadn't found much time for Internet dating, but then one day I knew I'd met the girl of my dreams when she replied to a comment I'd made on You-and-Me.com. She said, 'I love it when you talk equipment to me.'

Dan Jenkins

If a lot of people gripped a knife and fork the way they do a golf club, they'd starve to death.

Sam Snead

Relax? How can anybody relax and play golf? You have to grip the club, don't you?

Ben Hogan

People always say golfers don't smile. But there is so much psychology in golf so we have to be a bit robotic.

Lee Westwood

I'm thinking of taking up golf, but the idea of spending time with golfers frightens me.

Harlan Coben

Golfers don't scream. Golfers just adjust the pleats in their pants and go from there. That's about as antagonistic as we get.

Gary McCord

There are twice as many knitters as golfers in North America. Still, if you walk into any airport in North America, you can find a golf magazine but not a knitting magazine, even though you can't golf on a plane.

Stephanie Pearl-McPhee

I've never been one to
throw clubs, break clubs,
or use bad language on
the golf course. I've
played with golfers
who've done that, and
I really hate to see it.
If I did something like
that, my dad would come
get the putter and hit me
upside the head with it.
I knew better.

Lucas Black

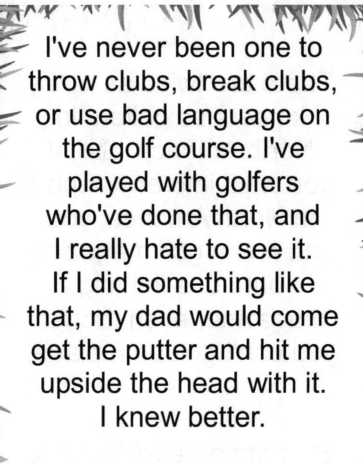

I play golf with friends sometimes, but there are never friendly games.

Ben Hogan

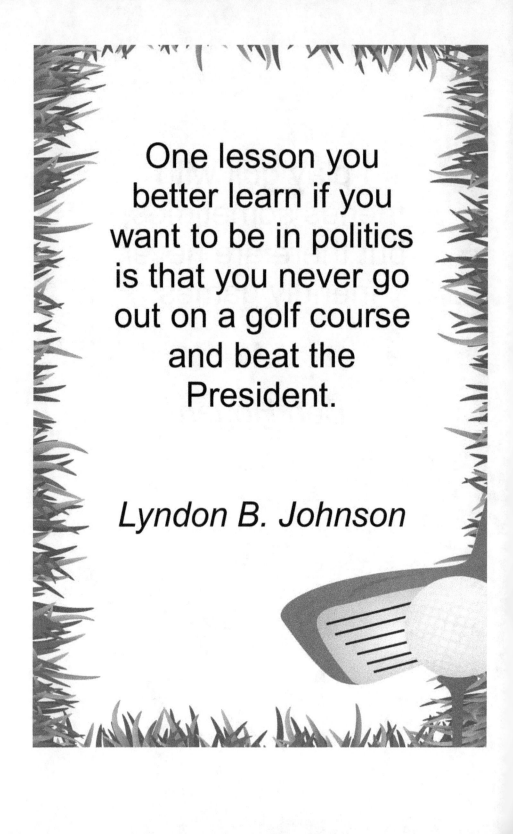

One lesson you
better learn if you
want to be in politics
is that you never go
out on a golf course
and beat the
President.

Lyndon B. Johnson

My first assistant-coaching job in football was at William & Mary in 1961. The pay wasn't much, so to get $300 more per year, I agreed to coach the golf team. I didn't even know how to keep score, and really, my main job was not to wreck the van on the way to tournaments.

Lou Holtz

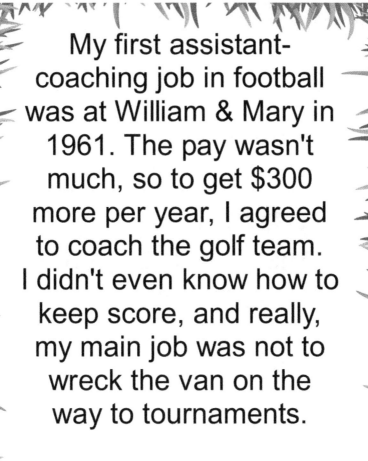

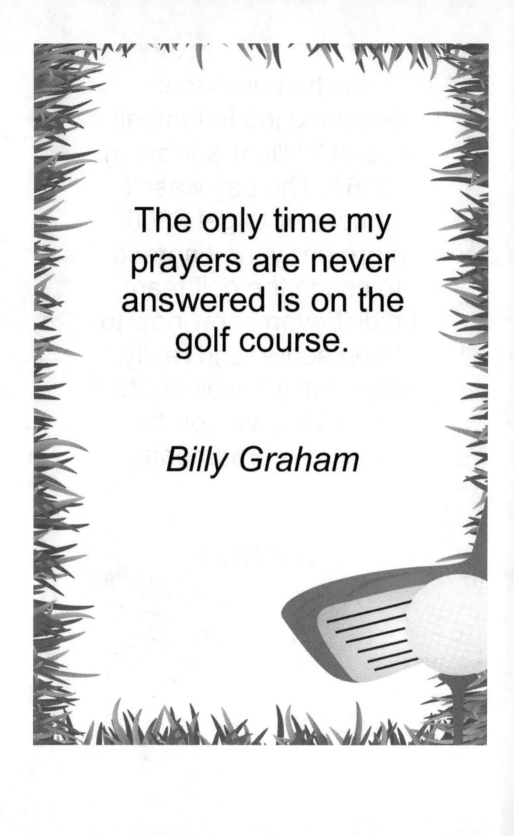

The only time my prayers are never answered is on the golf course.

Billy Graham

Somebody made the statement that Donald Trump has built or owns the greatest collection of golf courses, ever, in the history of golf. And I believe that is 100 percent true.

Donald Trump

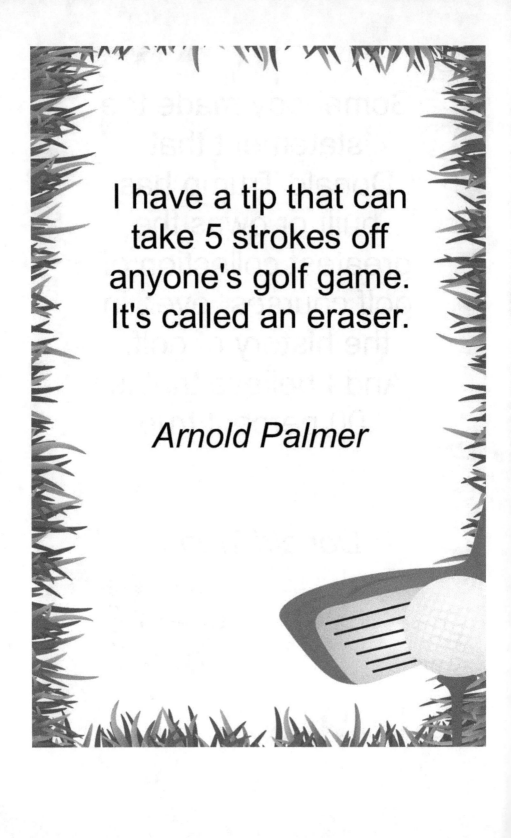

I have a tip that can take 5 strokes off anyone's golf game. It's called an eraser.

Arnold Palmer

Instead of saving for someone else's college education, I'm currently saving for a luxury retirement community replete with golf carts and handsome young male nurses who love butterscotch.

Jen Kirkman

Golf without bunkers
and hazards would
be tame and
monotonous.
So would life.

B. C. Forbes

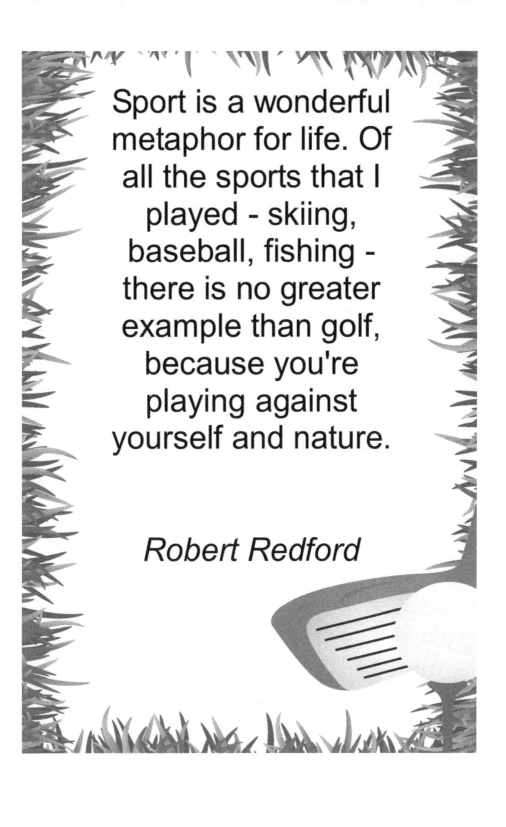

Sport is a wonderful metaphor for life. Of all the sports that I played - skiing, baseball, fishing - there is no greater example than golf, because you're playing against yourself and nature.

Robert Redford

The uglier a man's
legs are, the better
he plays golf -
it's almost a law.

H. G. Wells

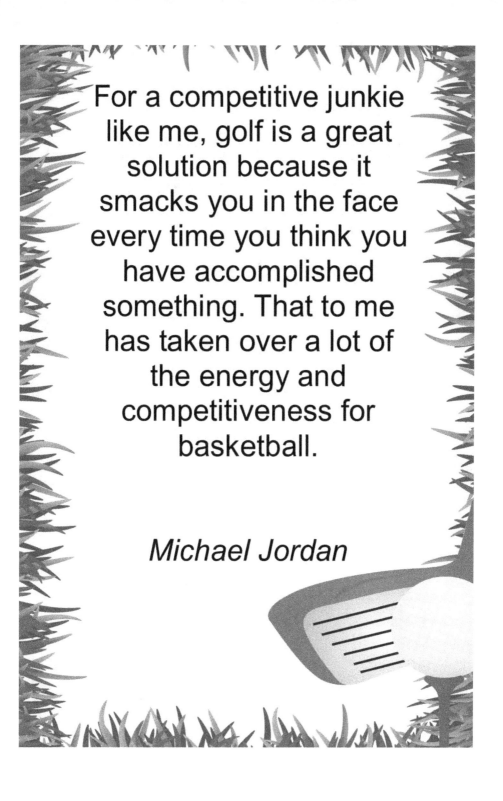

For a competitive junkie like me, golf is a great solution because it smacks you in the face every time you think you have accomplished something. That to me has taken over a lot of the energy and competitiveness for basketball.

Michael Jordan

It took me seventeen years to get three thousand hits in baseball. I did it in one afternoon on the golf course.

Hank Aaron

Golf is not a game of
good shots. It's a
game of bad shots.

Ben Hogan

Golf is fun - until you hit somebody in the head.

Charles Barkley

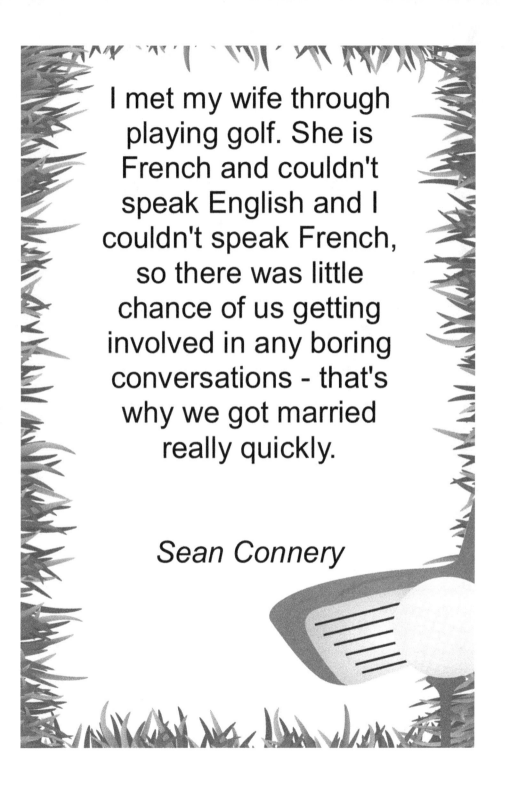

I met my wife through playing golf. She is French and couldn't speak English and I couldn't speak French, so there was little chance of us getting involved in any boring conversations - that's why we got married really quickly.

Sean Connery

Self-love is a big
part of golf.

Lewis Black

I think golf is literally an addiction. I'm surprised there's not Golf Anonymous.

Larry David

If there's a golf
course in heaven,
I hope it's like
Augusta National.
I just don't want an
early tee time.

Gary Player

To find a man's true character, play golf with him.

P. G. Wodehouse

I know I am getting
better at golf
because I am hitting
fewer spectators.

Gerald R. Ford

He who has the
fastest golf cart
never has a bad lie.

Mickey Mantle

I can't wait to be that age and hanging out with a bunch of people hanging out all day playing golf and going to the beach, all my own age. We'd be laughing and having a good time and getting loopy on our prescription drugs. Driving golf carts around. I can't wait.

Cameron Diaz

As we all know,
golf is a puzzle
without an answer.

Gary Player

The income tax has made liars out of more Americans than golf.

Will Rogers

While playing golf today I hit two good balls. I stepped on a rake.

Henny Youngman

What most people don't understand is that UFOs are on a cosmic tourist route. That's why they're always seen in Arizona, Scotland, and New Mexico. Another thing to consider is that all three of those destinations are good places to play golf. So there's possibly some connection between aliens and golf.

Alice Cooper

Golf is a good walk
spoiled.

Mark Twain

I'm 6' 6". It's hard to find golf clubs that fit you right and work right.

Charles Kelley

Golf is a day spent in a round of strenuous idleness.

William Wordsworth

I guess there is nothing that will get your mind off everything like golf. I have never been depressed enough to take up the game, but they say you get so sore at yourself you forget to hate your enemies.

Will Rogers

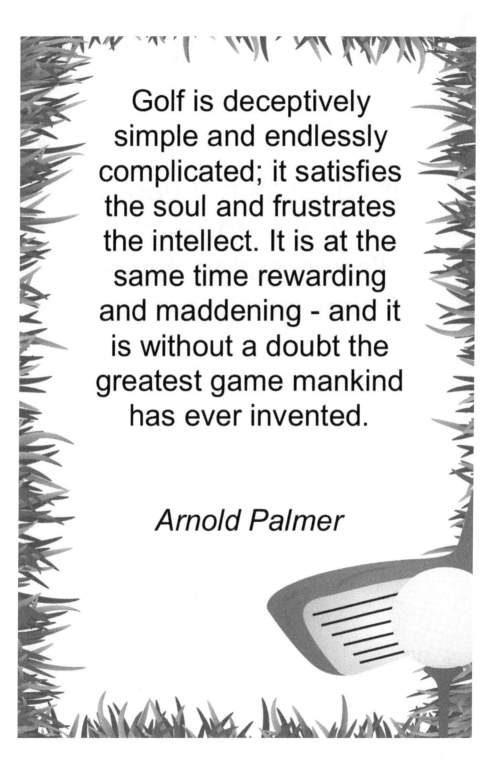

Golf is deceptively simple and endlessly complicated; it satisfies the soul and frustrates the intellect. It is at the same time rewarding and maddening - and it is without a doubt the greatest game mankind has ever invented.

Arnold Palmer

If you watch a game, it's fun. If you play it, it's recreation. If you work at it, it's golf.

Bob Hope

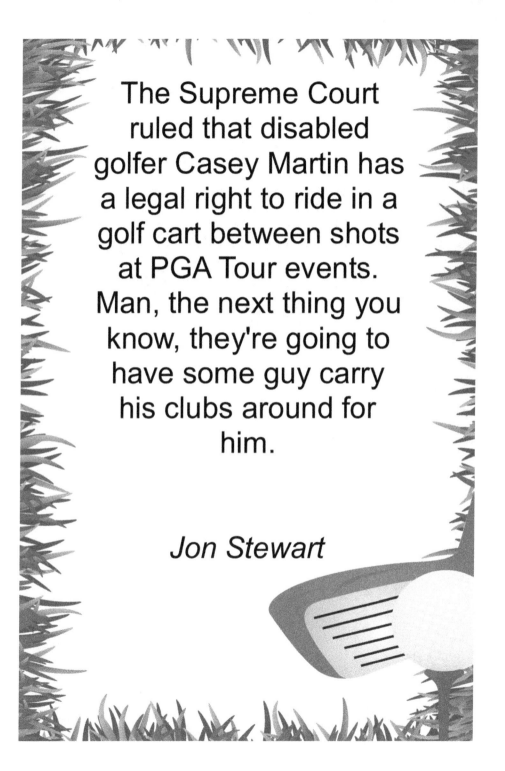

The Supreme Court ruled that disabled golfer Casey Martin has a legal right to ride in a golf cart between shots at PGA Tour events. Man, the next thing you know, they're going to have some guy carry his clubs around for him.

Jon Stewart

I'm not feeling very well - I need a doctor immediately. Ring the nearest golf course.

Groucho Marx

It's good sportsmanship to not pick up lost golf balls while they are still rolling.

Mark Twain

If you are caught on
a golf course during
a storm and are
afraid of lightning,
hold up a 1 iron.
Not even God can
hit a 1 iron.

Lee Trevino

As a kid, I might have been psycho, I guess, but I used to throw golf balls in the trees and try and somehow make par from them. I thought that was fun.

Tiger Woods

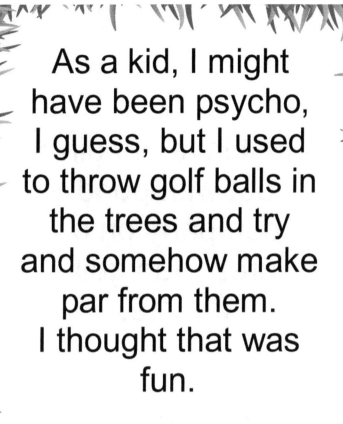

I just love hanging out with good company on a great, fun golf course.

Rich Eisen

Golf is so popular
simply because it is
the best game in
the world at which
to be bad.

A. A. Milne

CPSIA information can be obtained
at www.ICGtesting.com
Printed in the USA
LVHW080309240819
628845LV00023B/1129/P